613 DEP

LOUGHBOROUGH COLLEGE LIBRARY

AUTHOR: BUCKMAN, R.
TITLE: What you really need to know about living with depression
CI SMARK: 616.8527

be returned by the last date entered below.
erdue books.

What you really need to know abo...

LIVING WITH
DEPRESSION

Dr. Robert Buckman

with Anne Charlish

Introduced by John Cleese

D0795432

MARSHALL PUBLISHING

A Marshall Edition
Conceived by Marshall Editions
The Orangery
161 New Bond Street
London W1Y 9PA

First published in the UK in 2000 by
Marshall Publishing Ltd
Copyright © 2000 Marshall Editions Developments Ltd

All rights reserved. No part of this publication may be
reproduced, stored in a retrieval system, or transmitted, in any form
or by any means, electronic, mechanical, photocopying, recording or
otherwise, without prior written permission from the publisher.

ISBN: 1 84028 335 1

Originated in Italy by Articolor
Printed in and bound in Italy by Milanostampa

Managing Editor Linda Doeser
Indexer Susan Bosanko
Art Editor Siân Keogh
Illustrator Martin Laurie
Photographer David Jordan
Series Managing Editor Anne Yelland
Managing Art Editor Helen Spencer
Editorial Director Ellen Dupont
Art Director Dave Goodman
Editorial Coordinator Ros Highstead
Production Nikki Ingram, Anna Pauletti

LOUGHBOROUGH
COLLEGE
LIBRARY

Cover photography: front Superstock; back V.C.L./Telegraph Colour Library

Professor Brice Pitt MD BS, the consultant for this book, is a Fellow of the Royal College of
Psychiatrists. He has been a consultant psychiatrist at the Royal London Hospital and St
Bartholomew's Hospital. He is currently director of Hammersmith Hospital Memory Clinic and
the Emeritus Professor, Psychiatry of Old Age, Imperial College School of Medicine.

Every effort has been taken to ensure that all information in this book is correct and
compatible with national standards generally accepted at the time of publication.
This book is not intended to replace consultation with your doctor or other health professional.
The author and publisher disclaim any liability, loss, injury or damage incurred as a consequence,
directly or indirectly, of the use and application of the contents of this book.

Contents

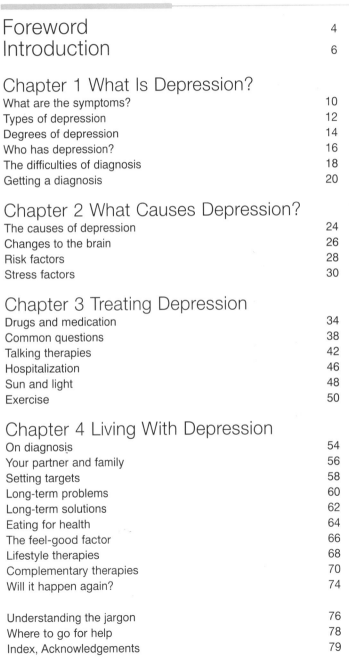

Foreword

Most of you know me best as someone who makes people laugh.

But for 30 years I have also been involved with communicating information. And one particular area in which communication often breaks down is the doctor/patient relationship. We have all come across doctors who fail to communicate clearly, using complex medical terms when a simple explanation would do, and dismiss us with a "come back in a month if you still feel unwell". Fortunately, I met Dr Robert Buckman.

Rob is one of North America's leading experts on cancer, but far more importantly he is a doctor who believes that hiding behind medical jargon is unhelpful and unprofessional. He wants his patients to understand what is wrong with them, and spends many hours with them—and their families and close friends—making sure they understand everything. Together we created a series of videos, with the jargon-free title *Videos for Patients*. Their success has prompted us to produce books that explore medical conditions in the same clear, simple terms.

This book is one of a series that will tell you all you need to know about your condition. It assumes nothing. If you have a helpful, honest, communicative doctor, you will find here the extra information that he or she simply may not have time to tell you. If you are less fortunate, this book will help to give you a much clearer picture of your situation.

More importantly—and this was a major factor in the success of the videos—you can access the information here again and again. Turn back, read over, until you really know what your doctor's diagnosis means.

In addition, because in the middle of a consultation, you may not think of everything you would like to ask your doctor, you can also use the book to help you formulate the questions you would like to discuss with him or her.

John Cleese

Introduction

DID YOU KNOW?

✓ However bad you feel now, you will get better. Depression can be cured.

✓ Treatment and help are available—for getting better faster.

Depression is one of the commonest medical conditions. In fact, it is estimated that one in four people will suffer from it at some times in their lives. It is more common than diabetes or asthma, yet it is also often poorly understood by those who have not suffered from it. The idea that depression is somehow your fault and that if you could only pull yourself together all would be well is still not uncommon. Often people suffering from depression do not realize it and attribute their physical symptoms, such as headaches and lethargy, to a physical cause. They then assume that their mental and emotional state is a response to a physical illness. They may even believe that somehow depression is not a real illness or, at least, not one to take seriously.

The fact that there are several different types of depression can make things even more confusing. In addition, there are many symptoms of depression, such as difficulty sleeping, feeling permanently tired, loss of libido, poor concentration or being irritable, that can be symptoms of other conditions or just temporary anomalies. This can mean that sometimes it is quite difficult to realize that you need help.

Getting help

Even if you—or a family member or close friend—recognize that you are depressed, you may still have doubts about how to get the help you need. You may feel frightened and unsure. Like many people, you may feel that you should struggle on in the belief that you will get better on your own. It's important to know that this is probably true; most depressed people do get better eventually even if they do nothing about their illness. For this reason, depression is described as a self-limiting illness. The problem is how you may feel while this is happening. Most headaches, for example, get better whether or not you take a painkiller. But most of us choose not to put up with pain when there's help at hand in the form of a pill. So it is with depression. Medication will usually speed your healing and help to relieve the unpleasant symptoms meanwhile. There are also a number of additional ways of helping you to cope with depression and speed up your recovery. Consult your doctor as soon as possible and start receiving the treatment that will lead to your recovery.

USING THIS BOOK

There are plenty of academic and medical books about depression that are of little use to the lay reader who wants help and understanding to come to terms with their depression—and to start feeling better. There are also lots of first-person accounts of depression and madness. And there are books of varying quality—some are excellent—aimed at the general market, but they are often much too long and simply too depressing. This book is intended to help you if you have been diagnosed as having depression, or you are close to someone who is suffering from depression. It's easy-to-follow, straightforward and reassuring. It describes how you may be feeling and will help you to realize that you are not alone. It tells you what your doctor may suggest and why, but, above all, it will let you know that there are a lot of people who can and will help you, who understand how you are feeling and can reassure you that you will recover.

Chapter

1

WHAT IS DEPRESSION?

What are the symptoms?

DOs AND DON'Ts

✓ Remember, you can be helped—consult your family doctor.

✗ Do not delay in consulting your doctor if you are preoccupied with ideas of suicide and death.

Classic depression, also called unipolar depression, is characterized by feelings of misery, anxiety and apathy. These main symptoms may help you spot depression.

Mental and emotional symptoms

Despondency and feeling low are typical of depression. Pessimism and a negative outlook are hallmarks. You may feel flat and tearful, unable to enjoy normally pleasurable activities, be indifferent to or irritable with your partner and children and feel generally miserable and hopeless. Crying for no apparent reason is common.

SYMPTOMS OF DEPRESSION

Many people suffering from depression are not able to understand what is happening to them or communicate their feelings to those closest to them. This chart is a check-list of some of the commonest symptoms.

SYMPTOM	CHARACTERISTICS
◆ GLOOM	◆ Pessimism, lack of humour, despondency, misery, despair
◆ ANXIETY	◆ Irritability, agitation, trembling, panic
◆ LOW SELF-ESTEEM	◆ Guilt, feelings of worthlessness
◆ APATHY	◆ Loss of interest and libido, tearfulness
◆ CONFUSION	◆ Poor concentration and memory, disorientation, alienation
◆ LOSS OF ENERGY	◆ Talking and walking in "slow motion", fatigue
◆ APPETITE CHANGES	◆ Usually a loss, sometimes an increase
◆ SLEEP CHANGES	◆ Early waking, difficulty in getting to sleep
◆ SUICIDAL FEELINGS	◆ Preoccupation with suicide and death

Anxiety can become so acute that you fear you are going mad. Perhaps, you simply "don't feel yourself". Things may look worse in the morning and improve as you force yourself to get on with the day. You may feel inadequate and a failure and think that you are a burden and a wet blanket, feeling guilty and blaming yourself when things go wrong. You may lose interest in things, including sex. You may feel tempted to stay in bed all day.

You may feel that your mental focus is poor and you are losing concentration. Your memory may start letting you down. A sense of disorientation and dislocation can be overwhelming, and a sense of dread and alienation may lead to panic.

Physical symptoms

Loss of energy is a typical symptom. You may feel drained, worn out and as if everything is too much effort. You may suffer from various aches and pains.

You may lose your appetite or, on the other hand, be eating more, snacking between meals and feeling a strong desire for carbohydrate. Your weight may start to increase or decrease for no obviously apparent reason, such as starting a diet or taking more exercise.

You may find it difficult to go to sleep at night, wake up repeatedly during the night or very early in the morning. You may feel tired throughout the day and unable to resist an afternoon sleep. You may want to go to bed much earlier than usual and sleep for longer.

Suicidal feelings

At worst, depressed people start to find every day a torment and begin for wish for a release. They become preoccupied with death and methods of suicide.

YOU REALLY NEED TO KNOW

◆ Changes in eating and sleeping patterns, combined with a loss of joy for life, are significant.

◆ Panic, anxiety, agitation, trembling, dizziness, fatigue, nausea, headache, aching limbs and lethargy are all signs of depression.

◆ If any of your friends talks of wanting to give up, and seems sad and "not themselves", they may be depressed.

◆ Never disregard someone who feels life is not worth living and talks of suicide.

Types of depression

✓ Learn to recognize your vulnerable times, such as the end of a relationship or a grey winter.

✗ Do not ignore self-destructive behaviour, such as drinking too much, reckless driving, smoking, compulsive gambling and compulsive spending.

Nowadays, doctors recognize four categories of depression in addition to classic depression, which is also known as unipolar illness. (For symptoms of classic depression see pp. 10–11.)

Manic depression (bipolar disorder)

Periods of depression and mania alternate. In mania, sufferers typically muster huge reserves of energy and may become productive. Their ideas may be wildly creative, even fanciful, and speech is rapid, but does not always making sense. Grandiose ideas are a hallmark.

When they are not severe, some sufferers enjoy the manic phases as they feel alive, obtain some relief and get a lot done. At its worst, mania precludes leading a normal life. Violent mood swings are the norm.

EXTREME MOOD SWINGS

People suffering from bipolar depression experience extreme swings in mood, from the lowest to the highest. If the mania is mild or moderate, the person can achieve a great deal and feels self-confident, even self-important. Energy levels are high and interest in sex is often considerable. When the mood swings to a low, then some of the symptoms of classic depression become apparent.

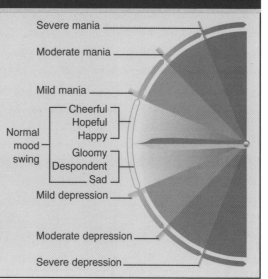

Severe mania

Moderate mania

Mild mania

Normal mood swing — Cheerful / Hopeful / Happy / Gloomy / Despondent / Sad

Mild depression

Moderate depression

Severe depression

Winter blues

Some people are profoundly biologically affected by winter's low light levels, resulting in Seasonal Affective Disorder (SAD). Symptoms include depression, fatigue, poor concentration and memory, increased appetite, particularly for carbohydrate, increased weight and a desire to sleep for longer than in the summer.

A true SAD sufferer so wants to sleep that he comes home from work, sleeps in front of the television, goes to bed late and falls asleep immediately and finds it difficult to get up in the morning. Other symptoms include feeling irritable, anxious, anti-social, miserable, guilty, lethargic and completely uninterested in sex.

Postnatal depression

"Baby blues" are common among new mothers. They tend to happen within five days of the birth and most women recover. Postnatal depression usually occurs later, even months after the birth. The symptoms are those of classic depression. The mother's misery, fear and anger may be directed at herself, her baby or both. Irritability, fatigue and sleeplessness are the hallmarks.

Puerperal psychosis is on a par with severe depression. The mother loses touch with reality and has delusions of being utterly bad. It may appear within weeks of the birth or not emerge for over a year.

Smiling depression

"I'm fine" can be a dangerously misleading response from people who manage to conceal their depression. These are the people who unexpectedly commit suicide. The desire to put on a brave face is strong, but the sufferer may snap without warning.

YOU REALLY NEED TO KNOW

◆ Smiling depression is especially insidious because the person suffering from it manages to conceal his misery beneath a cheerful exterior. This may be because he has already decided on the solution of suicide.

◆ Without treatment, the symptoms of depression tend to become more pronounced although, in the end, most people will recover spontaneously.

◆ Any new mother is at risk of postnatal depression—and those who have previously suffered with any type of depression are even more so.

Types of depression

Degrees of depression

✔ **Do see your doctor if you experience apathy, boredom, fatigue and a sense of "letting go".**

✔ **Do see your doctor if you habitually wake up in the middle of the night full of fear and dread, unable to get back to sleep.**

Mild depression

There is confusion in many people's minds about what is known in psychiatry and psychology as "understandable misery" (sadness with an identifiable cause) and mild depression. There is also much confusion, even these days, between being spineless and mild depression.

It is nearly 100 years since World War I when shell-shocked soldiers were shot, but old attitudes persist. Depression was not a recognized illness then. It is known now that a situation over which you have no control and cannot influence significantly increases the chances of depression. Mild depression falls into the categories of Levels 4 and 3 of the classification of psychiatric disorders (see Chart). See pp. 10–11 for symptoms.

Moderate depression

At this level, the symptoms intensify and it becomes increasingly difficult to function normally at home and at work. Depression at this level is categorized as neurosis: Level 2 in the Chart.

Severe depression

The sufferer loses touch with reality and cannot function normally. This may come into the category of psychosis, Level 1 in the Chart, but you can be severely depressed without being psychotic.

Reactive and endogenous depression

Depression used to be classified according to perceived origin. Reactive depression described a depression triggered by an external event, such as bereavement or divorce. Endogenous depression described low mood emanating from within and with no readily discernible cause. These distinctions are gradually being discarded because they are imprecise. The terms now in use are Major Depressive Disorder, Mood Disorder, Substance-induced Mood Disorder, Mood Disorder with Psychotic Features and Dysthymic Disorder.

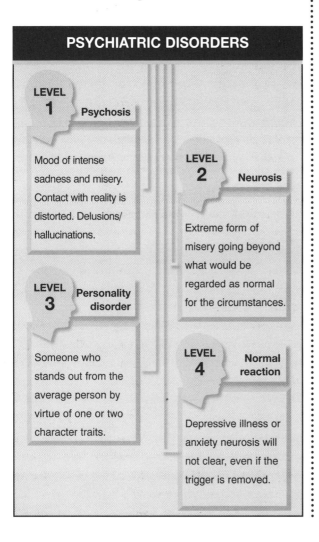

PSYCHIATRIC DISORDERS

LEVEL 1 **Psychosis**

Mood of intense sadness and misery. Contact with reality is distorted. Delusions/ hallucinations.

LEVEL 2 **Neurosis**

Extreme form of misery going beyond what would be regarded as normal for the circumstances.

LEVEL 3 **Personality disorder**

Someone who stands out from the average person by virtue of one or two character traits.

LEVEL 4 **Normal reaction**

Depressive illness or anxiety neurosis will not clear, even if the trigger is removed.

YOU REALLY NEED TO KNOW

◆ Many of us suffer with mild depression, which typically recurs.

◆ Symptoms vary considerably from one person to another, with some being more noticeable than others and some being absent altogether.

◆ Depression is curable—see Chapters 3 and 4.

Degrees of depress

Who has depression?

✓ The best outcome is a brief period of depression, which is successfully treated and does not return.

✗ The worst outcome is a complete depressive breakdown, followed by successive breakdowns and episodes of major depression.

Depression is twice as common as diabetes three times as common as cancer and more common than asthma. One in four people will suffer from some sort of mental illness at some time in their lives, while one in five people will suffer from depression.

At any one time about five percent (1 in 20) are suffering from severe depression. A further five percent of people are suffering from a milder form of depression.

Who are they?

◆ It is often said that five times more women than men suffer with depression. This is true in the case of mild depression, but for more severe depression the figures even out between women and men. Overall, depression is twice as common in women as in men.

◆ Depressed men are three times more likely than women to kill themselves.

AGE AND GENDER OF DEPRESSED PATIENTS

The chart shows the age groups and gender of patients treated for depression in the UK in 1998.

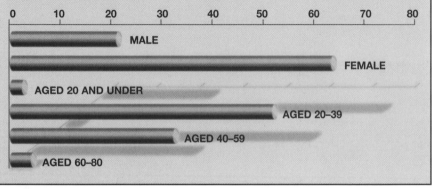

KEY FACTS

◆ Depression can affect anyone, regardless of status, wealth, education, profession or external events.

◆ At any given time, about 4–10 percent of women and 2–4 percent of men will be suffering from depression.

◆ Mothers of babies and young children.

◆ Depression occurs in 15 percent of people over the age of 65. The most severe forms of depression are more common in middle and old age. The highest suicide rates are among the elderly, particularly those aged over 75.

◆ People who have recently experienced a divorce, bereavement or other major life event, such as redundancy or moving house.

◆ Men in certain jobs, such as farmers (including horticulturists, farm managers and male farm workers), are twice as likely to commit suicide as the general population. Doctors, veterinary surgeons, pharmacists and dentists are also at particular risk.

◆ Adolescents (approximately three percent).

◆ Children (about one percent).

Are there other symptoms?

Among people suffering with depression, other symptoms are also common:

60–90 percent have symptoms of anxiety

30 percent suffer panic attacks

38 percent suffer obsessional symptoms

27 percent have social phobia

YOU REALLY NEED TO KNOW

◆ Depression can affect anyone from all age groups and all walks of life.

◆ Depression is a serious illness and has far-reaching consequences.

◆ Rapid, effective treatment lessens the chances of recurrence.

◆ Depression is common—in fact, one of the commonest of all medical conditions.

Difficulties of diagnosis

DIAGNOSIS

✓ Depression can be an illness in its own right, a secondary illness or part of a physical condition.

✗ Depression is not the result of an inadequate personality.

Depression is a complex illness for it can be an illness in its own right, it can be mistaken for other mental illnesses and it can also exist as part of physical disease. In addition, it can be mistaken for physical illnesses.

Even when depression exists in its own right and the primary diagnosis is depression, the anxiety associated with it may be so great that the family doctor diagnoses anxiety rather than depression. Panic attacks, obsessions and phobias are also common in depression.

Secondary illness

Depression can also exist as a secondary illness when the primary condition is agoraphobia, social phobia, substance abuse, alcoholism, obsessive-compulsive disorder, panic attack or anxiety. It is also common in many physical illnesses, especially stroke, cancer and

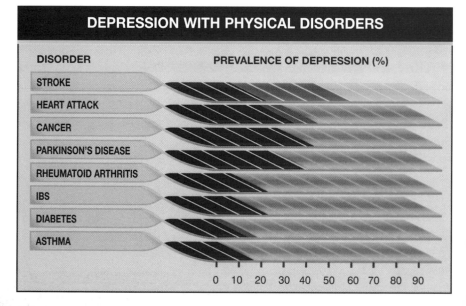

DEPRESSION WITH PHYSICAL DISORDERS

DISORDER	PREVALENCE OF DEPRESSION (%)
STROKE	
HEART ATTACK	
CANCER	
PARKINSON'S DISEASE	
RHEUMATOID ARTHRITIS	
IBS	
DIABETES	
ASTHMA	

0 10 20 30 40 50 60 70 80 90

SELF-MONITORING

◆ Keep a diary to record how you felt when you were depressed so that you may refer to it again in the event of a further episode.

◆ If you strongly believe that depression is only part of what you are suffering, you should persist with your family doctor and ask for a hospital referral. Ask for a second opinion if you are still not satisfied.

Parkinson's disease. It may also be associated with dementias and Alzheimer's disease. It is often seen in long-term illnesses, that is, chronic, disabling conditions such as heart disease and arthritis, and it is also common after 'flu.

Depression can be mistaken for thyroid disease, the onset of the menopause, glandular fever or the early stages of cancer when there are no signs other than pain to indicate cancer.

It is not your fault

Despite the fact that depression is a recognizable illness, many people, including some doctors, still believe that the symptoms amount to spinelessness, malingering, understandable misery or grief. "Pull yourself together" or "Get a grip on yourself" have become clichés simply because they are so often said by relatives or friends. No one who has ever suffered the fear and anguish of true depression would make that mistake. You are not to blame, but can take positive steps to recovery.

YOU REALLY NEED TO KNOW

◆ Anxiety, phobias and obsessive-compulsive disorder are often mistaken for depression.

◆ Depression can be wrongly diagnosed for some physical illnesses and it is, therefore, important that the relevant diagnostic tests are carried out.

◆ Even when it accompanies a major physical illness, depression still needs to be treated.

Difficulties of diagnosis

Getting a diagnosis

DOs AND DON'Ts

✓ See your doctor, ask questions and ask for a hospital referral if you are not satisfied.

✗ Don't blame yourself for being lazy or negative or assume that you have a physical illness if you feel depressed.

Your first visit will probably be to your family doctor. She may treat you herself or may refer you to a consultant psychiatrist. Alternatively, she may send you for various diagnostic tests in order to eliminate any physical illness. In this case, only when the results are received will she consider a psychiatric diagnosis.

If you are not satisfied with her diagnosis, be sure to ask for a referral to a hospital consultant. If you are not satisfied with the hospital consultant's diagnosis, you are within your rights to ask your family doctor for a second consultant opinion.

Asking the right questions

Doctors today expect their patients to ask questions, so don't be reluctant to do so. Remember, you have only a limited amount of time with the doctor and it is important to obtain the answers you are seeking. If it helps, write a list of your questions in advance.

REFERRAL

You may be referred to one of these specialists:

◆ Counsellor   ◆ Psychologist   ◆ Behavioural therapist

◆ Marital therapist   ◆ Cognitive therapist   ◆ Psychiatrist

◆ Psychotherapist

Each one can help by discussing your condition and problems with you in greater detail and at more length than the family doctor. Only the psychiatrist can prescribe medication. A psychiatrist is a medical doctor and can, therefore, prescribe drugs. Other specialists may not be doctors. (See Chapter 3.)

SELF-MONITORING

◆ If you strongly suspect a diagnosis yourself, do discuss it with your doctor.

◆ If you feel you are slipping into depression, consult your doctor without delay.

You may wish to ask some of the following.

- Why do I feel like this?
- What has caused it?
- How long will it go on for?
- Is it safe to drive?
- How long will the treatment take?
- Is it safe to take this treatment with the medication that I am already on (for another condition)?
- Will there be any side effects?
- What can I best do to help myself get better?
- When will I be able to go back to work?
- Does my employer have to know?

I'm not depressed!

Many people find it hard to believe a diagnosis of depression. This is not unusual. Even people who have been depressed before may be unable to believe that a second episode is upon them. One of the hallmarks of depression is losing your normal insight and mental focus. We may not realize how depressed we have become, particularly if it has come on slowly. We may think that we are being lazy or negative or that we have some other debilitating illness.

◆ The diagnosis of your condition and the reasons for the diagnosis.

◆ You can obtain a second opinion if you would like one.

◆ Depression is a recognizable illness and not merely being lazy or negative.

Chapter

2

WHAT CAUSES DEPRESSION?

Causes of depression

✓ Depression is an illness involving chemical changes in the brain.

✗ Cowardice, weak will, selfishness, laziness, flawed personality, self-indulgence, miserable disposition and faulty upbringing are not illnesses and are not the cause of depression.

The cause of depression is still not fully understood, although enough is known to treat it effectively. The distinguishing feature is lowered mood, but why that happens is not understood. It is known that the levels of certain brain chemicals fall in sufferers from depression, but it is not known why. The end of the twentieth century saw three main theories to explain the cause of depression: social, psychological and biological.

The social theory

In currency in the 1960s and 1970s, this theory is now generally discounted. Social psychiatrists believe that underlying personality traits are reinforced in the sufferer by major adverse life events that the sufferer cannot withstand and is overwhelmed by.

THE DOWNWARD SPIRAL

When someone is depressed, he may not feel up to doing very much, so achieves little if anything and then feels more depressed and worthless because nothing has been done. It is very easy to become trapped in this spiral and quite difficult to get out of it. It is important to value any positive actions, however small, and to realize that making an effort, not just the specific achievement, is valuable.

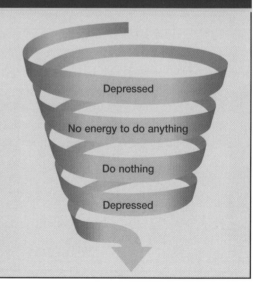

Depressed

No energy to do anything

Do nothing

Depressed

The psychological theory

This can be subdivided into three main categories: psychoanalytical, behavioural and cognitive. The first theory, now largely discredited, is based on the idea that unconscious feelings of aggression towards another person may be turned inward upon the sufferer.

The behavioural theory holds that the sufferer has learned that any action to improve life is pointless because too many adverse factors cannot be controlled.

The cognitive theory suggests that the depressed person has low expectations and so puts the most pessimistic interpretation possible upon any situation.

The biological theory

Dominant in the last two decades of the twentieth century and continuing to be so in the twenty-first, this theory suggests that depression is no different from, say, diabetes in that it results from a bodily irregularity—a brain chemical in the case of depression—that can be corrected with medication.

Other causes

The immediate cause of Seasonal Affective Disorder (winter blues) is low light levels but why this should trigger depression is not fully understood.

In postnatal depression, several stresses appear to act together: a previous history of depression, lack of emotional or practical support, a sick baby and—most significantly—plummeting levels of hormones.

Depression can also be caused by a number of prescribed drugs, including some for heart disease, steroids and decongestants, by some illnesses and infections and certain metabolic disorders.

YOU REALLY NEED TO KNOW

◆ What the person treating you believes the cause of your depression to be.

◆ Depression can be treated most effectively with medication and cognitive therapy—see Chapter 3.

◆ Depression has absolutely nothing to do with undesirable personality traits.

◆ Depression is probably caused by a number of factors and is not yet fully understood.

Changes to the brain

FACTS

✓ Depression is associated with changes in one or more chemicals in the brain.

✗ It is not known whether these changes are a cause or an effect of depression.

In depression, chemical changes occur in some pathways of the brain. These changes may vary with different forms of depression. However, it is not known whether these chemical changes cause depression or are one of the consequences of it.

In classic unipolar depression, the chemical changes may include alterations in the number or the sensitivity of nerve cell receptors for certain neurotransmitters (chemical messengers). The receptors for serotonin or 5HT (5-hydroxytryptamine), noradrenaline and dopamine, in particular, may be affected.

Serotonin or 5HT is involved in the regulation of mood and in maintaining normal patterns of appetite, sleep and sexual activity. Therefore, any abnormality in the 5HT pathways may lead to disturbance of sleep, increased anxiety and irritability and loss of sexual desire. These are all classic symptoms of depression.

GENETIC RISK FACTORS

◆ If one identical twin develops severe depression, the other has a 50 percent chance of becoming depressed.

◆ Depression in one non-identical twin signifies a 25 percent chance in the other of becoming depressed.

◆ The risk to children both of whose parents both suffer with depression is over 50 percent.

◆ Someone with a parent with manic depression has a 20 times greater chance of developing depression than someone whose parent does not have it.

◆ Postnatal depression is more likely in women who have a family medical history of depression.

◆ Depressed children have about four times the likelihood of developing depression in their adult lives.

Noradrenaline helps regulate mood and energy, both of which plummet in depression. Changes in the level of noradrenaline may lead to the overwhelming fatigue, loss of enthusiasm and social withdrawal that are characteristic of depression.

Dopamine plays a role in gaining pleasure and changes in this chemical messenger may therefore lead to the feeling that it is impossible to derive enjoyment from activities that you normally like. Abnormalities in dopamine may be especially important in people with manic depression (bipolar disorder).

Changes in all three of these neurotransmitters, known as monoamines, may be involved in depression. Other chemical messengers may also be associated with depression. Some evidence shows that changes within the brain are associated with the levels of certain hormones in the bloodstream.

It is not yet possible to test for the levels of all these chemicals in the brain, but it may become so in the future. A test for serotonin levels already exists, but it is crude and unreliable at present.

The genetic component

Certain genes also have an effect on depression, but the genetic picture remains unclear. Molecular biologists have, for some years, been confident of isolating the exact part of the gene or genes responsible for the development of depression. This knowledge will greatly help the development of new and better treatments.

It is known that depression runs in families, but it is not necessarily hereditary. It is simply that the risk is increased if depression already exists in the family, especially in parents or siblings.

YOU REALLY NEED TO KNOW

◆ Depression can be treated very effectively, even though its cause is not fully understood.

◆ If depression already exists in your family, you run a higher risk of developing it than someone who does not have a family history of depression.

Changes to the brain

Risk factors

DOs AND DON'Ts

✓ **Recognize the risk at stressful times and, if necessary, take pre-emptive action**

✗ **Don't keep on piling stress upon stress; try to stagger changes.**

The biggest risk factor of all for depression is loss. It may take the form of bereavement, divorce, moving house or the loss of a job. Stress of any sort is a well-recognized trigger for depression.

If a genetic disposition to depression does exist, it is clearly a risk factor. Anyone has a one in five (20 percent) chance of suffering with depression. The risk of both unipolar and bipolar disorder increases if you have a close relative, such as a parent, brother or sister, who suffers with depression.

YOUR STRESS RATING

The most commonly used rating for stress is that composed by Holmes and Rahe in 1967. Assess your stress rating by ticking the events you have experienced in the last year, then add together the figures for each life event:

LESS THAN 150

You have no more than the average risk of illness (30 percent).

150–299

You have a 50 percent probability of developing an illness.

OVER 300

You have an 80 percent chance of developing an illness.

If you have suffered with or have a predisposition for depression, the illness that you develop may prove to be depression.

Death of a spouse	100
Divorce	73
Marital separation	65
Prison term	63
Death of a close family member	63
Personal injury or illness	53
Marriage	50
Loss of job	47
Marital reconciliation	45
Retirement	45
Change in family member's health	44
Pregnancy	40
Sexual difficulties	39
Addition to family	39
Business readjustment	39
Change in financial state	38
Death of a close friend	37
Change to different type of work	36
More/fewer marital arguments	35
Taking out a large mortgage or loan	31
Foreclosure on mortgage or loan	30
Change in work responsibilities	29

The winter risk

Sufferers from Seasonal Affective Disorder are clearly at risk with the onset of autumn and winter and the decreasing levels of natural light. You can lower this risk by using a special light box every morning from the autumn onwards (see pp. 48–9). This device gives out bright light at a particular wavelength and not only cures the depression of most SAD sufferers, but is also an effective method of preventing a yearly recurrence, once an initial diagnosis has been made.

Son or daughter leaving home	29
Trouble with in-laws	29
Outstanding personal achievement	28
Spouse begins or stops work	26
Starting or finishing school	26
Change in living conditions	25
Change of personal habits	24
Trouble with boss	23
Change in work hours or conditions	20
Change in residence	20
Change in school	20
Change in recreational habits	19
Change in church activities	19
Change in social activities	18
Taking out a small mortgage or loan	17
Change in sleeping habits	16
More/fewer family gatherings	15
Change in eating habits	15
Holiday	13
Christmas	12
Minor violation of the law	11

YOU REALLY NEED TO KNOW

◆ Exactly how vulnerable you are.

◆ When you are most likely to be at risk.

◆ Depression can and does recur.

◆ Even happy events, such as getting married, cause stress.

Risk factors

Stress factors

DOs AND DON'Ts

✓ Do take a whole day for yourself and give yourself essential breathing space.

✗ Don't turn down offers of practical help with stressful tasks, such as moving house or caring for young children.

Individual variation

How people tolerate stress in their lives varies greatly from one individual to another. Some people can tolerate losing their job, selling their house and having a baby all in the same year without succumbing to depression. Other more vulnerable individuals may find that the break-up of a relationship and a change of job is more than they can withstand before falling ill. This has nothing to do with moral fibre. It is simply a matter of how psychologically robust each individual may be. What is important is to recognize your own limits in order to avoid piling stress upon stress.

Try to take some time for yourself, however busy your lifestyle. It is especially important to have a pause and relax when you know that a stressful event is ahead.

HEIGHTENING THE RISK

All these factors, separately or in combination, further add to your risk of becoming depressed:

◆ Coming from an economically poor background

◆ Being unable to confide in your partner

◆ Having a poor social life, especially in later life

◆ The experience of rejection by parents in childhood

◆ Perfectionism

◆ Anxiety

◆ Illness or surgery

◆ Poor diet

◆ Several young children at home

◆ Drinking alcohol to excess

Recognizing risk

If you start to feel that everything has got on top of you, make arrangements for Time Out. Cancel all appointments and commitments for one day. Put on the answerphone. Arrange for someone to take care of your children—there must be at least one friend or relative who lives nearby and would help out. Just do nothing for one whole day and get your breath back. This short pause in a stressful life can help to lessen the chances of developing a depressive illness.

YOU REALLY NEED TO KNOW

◆ Your own limits, so that you can take steps to prevent stresses building up to such an extent that depression results.

◆ Taking a short break in a demanding life from time to time lessens stress and so reduces the chances of developing depression.

Chapter

3

TREATING DEPRESSION

Drugs and medication

✔ Do monitor your mental and physical reactions to new medication.

✗ Don't stop taking the medication as soon as you start to feel better.

Many people believe that drugs for treating depression are addictive and so are reluctant to take them. Some of the drugs used in the past were addictive, but the anti-depressants in general use today are not habit-forming. Sleeping tablets and anti-anxiety drugs, also known as tranquillizers, however, are potentially addictive.

Some people are reluctant to take medication for depression because they do not like the idea of needing a "crutch" and believe that they should be able to manage without medication. However, if you had a headache, you would probably take an aspirin, even though you knew it would eventually go away. The more we learn about the illness of depression, the more we realize that it is associated with a biological deficiency, which can be effectively treated with medication.

Tricyclic anti-depressants

These include imipramine, amitriptyline, nortriptyline, clomipramine, protriptyline, doxepin, trimipramine, dothiepin and lofepramine. Each has its own specific characteristics and differs in some ways from the others.The TCAs were developed in 1958.

TYPES OF MEDICATION

◆ Anti-depressants

◆ Lithium to treat mania

◆ Sleeping tablets

◆ Anti-anxiety drugs (known as anxiolytics/tranquillizers)

TCAs can take anything from a week to several weeks to work and length of treatment varies. They work by correcting a deficiency of monoamines in the brain. These are chemical transmitters and their levels become reduced during depression.

Because they are cheap, TCAs are often the first drug prescribed. However, they have some unpleasant side effects and so may not be your doctor's first choice. But if you are one of the people who does not respond to other drugs, they may prove effective. Side effects may include difficulty urinating, constipation, rapid heartbeat, feeling faint, drowsiness and confusion. If they are prescribed, your doctor will supervise their use.

There are few withdrawal symptoms, although there may be a relapse into depression a few weeks later.

Monoamine oxidase inhibitors

MAOIs include phenelzine, tranylcypromine and moclobemide. They are so called because they slow down the removal of monoamines by the enzyme monoamine oxidase. Each drug has its own specific characteristics and no two are identical. They were developed in the late 1950s/early 1960s. The first was actually a treatment for tuberculosis, which was then found to improve mood—a happy, accidental discovery.

They can take a few weeks to work and the length of treatment varies. There is no doubt that they work, but they have many side effects, including lowered blood pressure leading to dizziness and fainting, headaches and sleep problems. Some of this family of drugs may interact adversely with foods such as mature cheese and pickled fish, so make sure your doctor advises you about which foods to avoid.

YOU REALLY NEED TO KNOW

◆ Anti-depressants are not addictive.

◆ Anti-depressants are very effective.

◆ Depression is entirely curable through the use of medication.

Drugs and medication

Drugs and medication

✓ Consult your doctor without delay if you experience any worrying side effects.

✗ If feelings of suicidal despair persist for several weeks after you have started the medication, don't ignore them; consult your doctor.

Selective serotonin reuptake inhibitors

The best-known SSRIs are fluoxetine (under the brand name Prozac) and paroxetine (Seroxat in the UK and Paxil in the USA). Others are citalopram, fluvoxamine, paroxetine (Seroxat) and sertraline. Each drug in the SSRI family has its own characteristics and no two are identical. For example, Seroxat is usually more effective than Prozac in treating depression accompanied by an element of obsessive-compulsive disorder.

SSRIs are so called because they raise serotonin levels in the brain. These levels are lower than normal in people with depression. The length of treatment varies from person to person. Many people suffering from depression have found them very helpful. They are just as effective as the TCAs, but without the worrying side effects of the older drugs.

Nevertheless, you may be unlucky enough to experience nausea, insomnia and general agitation or anxiety. Some people lose their sex drive.

THE NEW ANTI-DEPRESSANTS

Newer types of drugs, which are more selective and more specific than the SSRIs and which have fewer side effects, are gradually coming into use.

◆ NARIs (noradrenaline reuptake inhibitors), the first one of which, reboxetine, became available in the UK in 1998

◆ A number of drugs which are at trial stage now will be introduced within the next ten years

◆ SNRIs (serotonin-noradrenaline reuptake inhibitors), such as venlafaxine (introduced in 1995 and used to treat resistant depression) and milnacipran

◆ SRMs (serotonin receptor modulators)

Lithium

Lithium carbonate (often simply called lithium) is a mood regulator and the drug your doctor will usually choose if you are suffering from mania and manic depression. Other drugs he might prescribe include carbamazepine and sodium valproate.

It may take several months before it is fully effective. Your doctor will arrange regular tests to monitor the amount of lithium in your blood because the level required for the treatment to work is not much below the toxic level. Since you might experience some unpleasant side effects, such as reduced thyroid function, thirst, trembling, nausea and diarrhoea, your doctor will supervise its use. Lithium is sometimes prescribed in combination with TCAs. Carbamazepine and sodium valproate also may have serious side effects.

Sleeping tablets

Insomnia and waking in the early hours of the morning, both common signs of depression, can be treated with sleeping tablets. If you take them for only a short time while you are completely exhausted, they can be very helpful. However, most of these drugs are addictive, so you should not take them for more than two weeks. Think of them as a short-term bridge.

Anti-anxiety drugs

Anxiety is a very common feature of depression and your doctor may prescribe anti-anxiety drugs, or tranquillizers, to help you in the weeks that it can take for anti-depressant medication to become effective. Some anxiolytics are addictive, so, as with sleeping tablets, your doctor will prescribe them for short-term use only.

YOU REALLY NEED TO KNOW

◆ You should consult your doctor when you intend to stop taking medication and follow guidelines in order to minimize any possible withdrawal symptoms.

◆ Most sleeping tablets and some anxiolytics are addictive and are for short-term use only.

◆ Some anti-depressants, such as TCAs like amitriptyline and trimipramine, are quite sedative. If you take them at night, they work as sleeping tablets first and as anti-depressants later.

Common questions

DOs AND DON'Ts

✓ If you can, report all side effects, if any, to your doctor without delay, however unimportant you think they are.

✗ Do not continue with medication which makes you feel no different and from which you are deriving no benefit— consult your doctor.

Anti-depressants do not actually cure the condition of depression. However, anti-depressant medication is valuable and effective in that it eliminates the biological symptoms of depression, in turn alleviating the dreadful psychological symptoms, with the result that you will feel very much better.

How long before they work?

Your individual makeup, the degree of depression, the dosage and whether you are taking other prescribed drugs (which may induce depression) will affect the time it takes for anti-depressants to work. You will probably notice some beneficial effects within one to two weeks, but it may take a month for them to become fully effective. As a rule, if an anti-depressant has shown no benefit within six weeks, your doctor may suggest another drug. It is important to take anti-depressant drugs regularly, as they need to build up in the body.

How long do I need to take them for?

The intensity of your depression, your medical history and current circumstances and whether this is the first episode of the illness will all have a bearing on the length of treatment. About 30 percent, some say 50 percent, of people experience a recurrence if they stop their medication after six months. This figure drops to only two percent if the medication is continued for one year.

What are the possible side effects?

After reading the information accompanying the medication, you may be tempted not to take it. But we all have to make choices and you must look at the risk-benefit ratio. Essentially, are the benefits worth the risks?

POSSIBLE SIDE EFFECTS

MAOIs

Dizziness, fainting, headaches, insomnia, lowered blood pressure–some react with certain foods

SSRIs

Agitation, anxiety, insomnia, lowered or absent sex drive, nausea

TCAs

Confusion constipation,difficulty passing water, drowsiness, feeling faint, rapid heartbeat

If you feel apathetic, can't sleep, are irritable with your children and partner, despairing and occasionally suicidal, you may well conclude that some initial nausea or excessive sweating, for example, is a good swap for the absolute misery of the previous weeks or months.

The possible side effects of anti-depressants depend on the type of drug, the specific drug and your individual response. Some drugs, notably the TCAs and MAOIs, will probably produce the same common side effects in most people, plus some rarer ones in some people but not others. Some people experience side effects with SSRIs, while others do not. Of those who do, some can tolerate them, while others either cannot or choose not to and ask for an alternative drug.

You should report all side effects, whether or not you consider them important and whether or not you can tolerate them, to your doctor. This is important for your health and for feedback to the pharmaceutical industry.

YOU REALLY NEED TO KNOW

◆ The benefits of feeling better often outweigh the possible side effects of anti-depressants.

◆ The World Health Organization (WHO) recommends that treatment for depression should continue for at least six months after the symptoms have improved or disappeared.

Common questions

DOs AND DON'Ts

✓ Avoid alcohol or at least cut down on it if you are taking any medication.

✗ Don't stop taking the medication suddenly without medical supervision.

Is it safe to drive?

It is normally safe to drive a car, but if you feel drowsy, confused, agitated or unusually anxious, don't drive until these side effects wear off. You will be the first to notice if your reactions are slower or more nervous than normal. If in doubt about driving, don't.

Sleeping tablets and tranquillizers slow the reactions, so take extra care when driving if you have taken either of these types of medication in the last few days.

Is it all right to drink alcohol?

Some drugs interact with alcohol. Check with your doctor, but it would be wise to cut down on alcohol so that you can observe any side effects. Also, alcohol acts initially like a stimulant and then as a depressant so it is best avoided when you are depressed. Do not drink alcohol if you are taking sleeping tablets or anxiolytics.

It takes a little time for anti-depressants to start to work, but once the levels in your body have built up, you will quickly begin to feel better, more energetic and interested in things.

Why must I keep on taking them?

To have a lasting effect, anti-depressant medication must be taken for the full course. Research shows that the chances of relapse and recurrence are substantially higher the earlier the course is terminated.

Depression is normally the result of certain hormonal changes in the body and brain. These are associated with changes in the sensitivity of receptors on which these hormones work. Anti-depressants allow more of these hormones to accumulate, forcing over-sensitive receptors back to their normal level. This takes several weeks which is why anti-depressants do not appear to work straight away and why there may be a delay before there is any outward sign of improvement.

What happens when I stop?

Your doctor will advise you about tapering off the medication gradually and about withdrawal symptoms and how to cope with them. You should not stop the medication suddenly without medical supervision.

What are the alternatives?

There is little alternative to medication for people who are severely depressed or psychotic, except for psychosurgery and electroconvulsive therapy (ECT). Anti-depressant medication works better than most other treatments. For those with mild to moderate depression, alternative treatments include the talking therapies, psychotherapy (pp. 42–5), sunlight and light therapy for sufferers from SAD (pp. 48–9), exercise (pp. 50–1) and the complementary therapies (pp. 68–73). However, mildly to moderately depressed people may still get better more quickly on medication than without.

◆ 60–70 percent of depressed people will get better within six to eight weeks if they take anti-depressant medicine.

◆ Stopping the medication too early or giving it up is the most common cause of failure to get better from depression.

Talking therapies

DOs AND DON'Ts

✓ Keep a diary to record your feelings at the end of each therapy session and assess your progress at the end of each month.

✗ Do not give up if you do not feel at ease with and respect your therapist; seek a different one by consulting your family doctor.

One common feature of all psychotherapies is the therapist's belief that she will be able to help modify your feelings, views and ideas about yourself by counselling. A second common feature is that she is not there to find answers to your problems, but to allow you to find your own answers through the technique of exploratory discussion. By developing your own strategies, you will gain in maturity and strength, so forming the foundations for managing your future life.

Psychotherapy is far from being an easy option. It requires motivation, commitment, time and money. It can be emotionally painful but it can prove rewarding and of long-term emotional benefit. Psychotherapy is said to be most effective when combined with medication.

Supportive psychotherapy

Talking to a friend when you are depressed can be of inestimable value. Some forms of psychotherapy are similar, with the therapist not expected to find solutions or make judgements. Supportive psychotherapy enables

Talking to a sympathetic and non-judgmental professional enables you to air your feelings, problems and worries freely and, through discussion, to work out your own strategies and solutions.

TYPES OF THERAPY

- ◆ Supportive psychotherapy
- ◆ Interpersonal therapy
- ◆ Behavioural therapy
- ◆ Group therapy
- ◆ Marital therapy
- ◆ Psychoanalysis
- ◆ Cognitive therapy

you to air your problems as you perceive them to a sympathetic ear. This is a necessary element in helping anyone recover from depression and, ideally, also forms part of any medical consultation for any illness. Many different health professionals are trained to offer this help, including doctors, specialist nurses, counsellors, psychologists and health visitors.

Behavioural therapy

People with a phobia can find behavioural therapy helpful. You are gradually exposed to the feared object or situation and shown that you will not come to harm. You learn techniques for dealing with anxiety and panic. After increasingly close encounters with the object of the phobia, you will gain confidence in dealing with it.

Marital therapy

If you feel that the roots of your depression lie in your relationship with your partner, marital therapy may be suggested. This gives you both the opportunity to air your grievances, without fear of recrimination, in the presence of an objective third party.

YOU REALLY NEED TO KNOW

◆ It is important to talk to someone about your problems and about how you feel.

◆ Everything that you discuss with or tell to a professional therapist remains confidential, just as it does with your family doctor.

◆ Marital therapy is not always focused on reconciliation; it may, in some cases, be used to help each partner to accept separation without bitterness.

Talking therapies

Talking therapies

DOs AND DON'Ts

✓ Consult your doctor to find the right talking cure and the appropriate therapy for your depression.

✗ Do not stop taking your medication when you begin a talking therapy; they work best together.

Cognitive therapy

Together with interpersonal therapy (see below), cognitive therapy is at the cutting edge of modern psychotherapies. Cognition describes thinking, memory and perception. Cognitive therapy may be defined as help with how we view events and situations. It works on the basis that as how we think determines how we feel, by modifying our automatic reactions and thoughts, our feelings and moods will be altered.

The aim of this therapy in treating depression is to identify and challenge negative and pessimistic thought patterns with a view to developing more realistic and more objective thoughts. These, by definition, are more optimistic, so your mood improves and your depression starts to lift. If you try cognitive therapy, you will be encouraged to keep a diary to record your moods, thoughts and activities, to challenge stereotypical behaviour, to set targets and carry out self-help tasks as homework and to instigate a system of rewards for each small positive step and achievement.

This therapy is especially suitable for problems of low self-esteem and for patterns of destructive behaviour, such as uncontrollable anger, compulsive gambling and alcoholism. It is most useful for people with recurrent depression who have developed a negative and self-defeating way of thinking about themselves so that any adversity can provoke a severe depression.

Interpersonal therapy

Aimed at improving personal relationships, interpersonal therapy is based on the view that the crucial factor in depression is your social network or interpersonal relationships. These are determined, to some extent, by

PSYCHOANALYSIS

Now less widely used, this therapy was developed by Sigmund Freud. However, psychotherapy based on psychoanalytic theory does help many people to understand their present behaviour in terms of past experience and emotions. In dynamic psychotherapy, the depressed person develops feelings about the therapist that are used to revive past feelings towards his parents.

YOU REALLY NEED TO KNOW

◆ Many support groups—Alcoholics Anonymous, slimmers' groups, quit-smoking groups and compulsive shoppers' groups— use the principles of group therapy.

◆ All talking cures require time and commitment from you and from the therapist.

life events and parental relationships. Three themes can commonly be seen in people with depression: a failure to achieve a safe and harmonious relationship with their parents despite attempts, the experience of being told repeatedly that they are stupid, naughty, unlovable or incompetent and the loss of a parent while still a child.

Interpersonal therapy can help you to explore your reactions to grief and loss, conflicts with friends, family and colleagues, your social skills and any problems you may have of adjusting to major life changes— bereavement, divorce, retirement—with a view to modifying your perceptions.

Group therapy

A group of people, united by the similarity of their problems, can be given psychotherapy together. This can prove helpful in that it shows you that you are not alone and that others are in a somewhat similar situation. Each member can contribute to the progress and well-being of the others by posing questions, offering constructive criticism, appraisal and encouragement.

Hospitalization

✓ However bad you feel about being in hospital, always remember that depression is curable and you will get better.

✗ Don't be put off by out-of-date images of psychiatric wards — modern psychiatric wards are nothing like those of the past.

Hospital treatment can be beneficial because doctors can make a more rigorous assessment of your condition, so they can offer the most appropriate treatments. They will also receive feedback from the nurses on the ward and others involved in your care. On the other hand, admission will disrupt your life. In the case of severely depressed or psychotic patients, who may constitute a threat to others or themselves, it may be the only sensible course until their condition has improved.

Psychiatric in-patients can be given higher doses of anti-depressants and anxiolytics than out-patients. Side effects can be continuously monitored and the patient's condition regularly observed.

Electroconvulsive therapy (ECT)

This treatment can work well in cases of recurrent severe depression that resist treatment with medication and psychotherapy and in which there is a high risk of suicide. The patient is given a short-acting anaesthetic, a muscle relaxant and oxygen ventilation before an

WHY SOME PEOPLE NEED TO STAY IN HOSPITAL

◆ They pose a threat to themselves or to other people.

◆ They require increased medication or medication with troublesome side effects.

◆ They need intensive psychotherapy and support, for example, in cases of severe postnatal depression.

◆ ECT, which can be an effective treatment for the severely depressed where other treatments have failed, can only be administered in hospital.

◆ Psychosurgery may be required for someone with severe, recurrent depression when other treatments have failed.

THOSE CARING FOR YOU

CONSULTANT PSYCHIATRIST

You will be under the care of a senior doctor with an additional qualification in psychiatry, but you may not see him every day.

PSYCHIATRIST

With the same qualifications as the consultant, but at a more junior level, this doctor is likely to take responsibility for your day-to-day treatment

PSYCHOLOGIST

This member of the team has a degree in psychology and may or may not be a medical doctor.

PSYCHIATRIC NURSE

Nurses specializing in psychiatry will be on hand as your first point of contact throughout the day and night.

PSYCHOTHERAPIST (see pp. 42–5)

(see pp. 42–5)

electric current is passed through the brain via electrodes. This induces a fit lasting about 30 seconds. The treatment may be repeated several times within a week and for several weeks. There may be some temporary memory loss.

Psychosurgery

Surgery uses short-acting radioactive isotopes to produce lesions in those parts of the brain involved in the process of depression. Recovery is usually quick—within a couple of days. It is now very rarely performed.

YOU REALLY NEED TO KNOW

◆ You can accept or decline treatment in consultation with your psychiatrist. Even if you have been legally detained, you can still discuss the merits and risks of treatment with those responsible for your care. You have the right of appeal.

◆ You can accept or decline visitors.

◆ Stringent guidelines for administering ECT are adhered to and were developed in response to criticisms of the treatment when it was first introduced.

Hospitalization

Sun and light

DOs AND DON'Ts

✓ Increase your length of exposure if you seem to be deriving little benefit.

✗ If you start to feel irritable and over-active, decrease your amount of exposure to light.

Do you sometimes feel depressed, sluggish and inclined to nibble on sugary, carbohydrate snacks, such as cakes and biscuits? Do you tend to experience this during the late winter and early spring months? Do you usually welcome the spring and the summer months? If the answer to each of these questions is yes, you would probably benefit from light therapy.

Most of us usually feel better in the summer months when light levels are higher than in the winter months. Our mood lifts, colours become more vibrant, everything springs into life. A week's holiday in the sun during the winter months can significantly relieve depression— although the effect is, unfortunately, not long lasting.

MELATONIN PRODUCTION

The pineal gland in the brain secretes a hormone called melatonin, which is derived from serotonin. It is linked to the cycle of day and night, is involved in regulating bodily functions and is what causes animals to hibernate. Sunlight stops the production of melatonin. The weaker light of winter often does not reach a sufficiently high level, so melatonin production is not suppressed and susceptible people develop SAD.

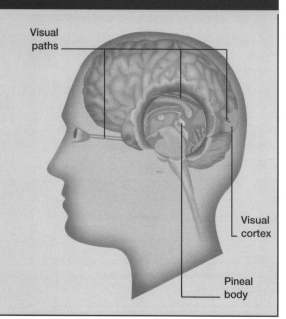

Visual paths

Visual cortex

Pineal body

Light therapy is a happy combination of harnessing natural forces with applied scientific research.

Seasonal Affective Disorder

Winter depression may be caused by a rise in the level of melatonin, a substance produced in the brain. When light levels are increased, the production of melatonin stops and the depression lifts. The significance of low light levels was not recognized until the start of the 1980s. Research identified what is now known as Seasonal Affective Disorder, SAD (see Chapter 1).

The results of using light therapy at trial stage in the early 1980s were spectacular: up to 80 percent of people who had fallen into a devastating depression every winter for years were suddenly, within a week, cured of their depression with no serious side effects. They reported lifting of the depression, good mood and soaring energy levels.

All you have to do is look at a light box from anything from 30 minutes to up to four or five hours, depending on the intensity of the box used and on the severity of depression. You can continue to work, read or watch television while looking at the light box.

YOU REALLY NEED TO KNOW

◆ Sunlight and artificial light of sufficient intensity relieve depression in less than a week in 75–80 percent of people with SAD.

◆ If you obtain a box of 10,000 lux, you will probably need only 30 minutes' exposure each day.

◆ Light therapy still works successfully through spectacles and contact lenses.

◆ Some light boxes are portable and some are designed so that you can continue working, reading or watching television while absorbing light.

◆ Ordinary domestic electric lights are not intense enough to affect hormonal changes in the body.

Exercise

DOs AND DON'Ts

✓ **Try to walk for up to an hour each day and to take regular vigorous exercise several times a week.**

✗ **Do not let yourself invent excuses to avoid taking exercise.**

Many people have learned for themselves to keep depression at bay through regular exercise. They know that they continue to feel good if they exercise regularly and that their mood soon plummets if they cannot do so. They may not know that this is because exercise may increase levels of mood-raising endorphins in the brain.

Exercise is now so widely recognized to be beneficial, that some depressed patients are given vouchers for leisure centres on the NHS so that they can take regular exercise at aerobic classes or swimming. As well as being beneficial for depression, exercise also relieves anxiety, a common component of depression.

Walking and swimming are the best all-round forms of exercise and may be the easiest to incorporate into a busy life. However, many other forms of exercise, from dancing to yoga, may prove appealing.

CHOOSE THE RIGHT EXERCISE FOR YOU

◆ Aerobics	◆ Football	◆ Skipping
◆ Aquarobics	◆ Golf	◆ Squash
◆ Badminton	◆ Jogging	◆ Step class
◆ Belly dancing	◆ Line dancing	◆ Tai Chi
◆ Circuit training	◆ Riding	◆ Tennis
◆ Cycling	◆ Rowing	◆ Windsurfing
◆ Dance exercise class	◆ Rugby	◆ Weight training
◆ Exercise class	◆ Salsa dancing	◆ Yoga

For how long?

A brisk walk in the fresh air for 30–60 minutes every day will do much to keep you fit and happy. If you can do some sort of vigorous exercise three to five times a week for a minimum of 30 minutes a session, you are sure to feel better, both mentally and physically.

Good air quality and sunlight will increase the benefits of the exercise that you decide upon. Outdoor exercise of any type is ideal for banishing sluggishness and for getting good fresh oxygen into your lungs.

Overcoming obstacles

You may say, I don't have time, I don't have the right equipment, I can't afford it. However, there is always a solution to every problem—in this case, walking. You don't need any special equipment, it doesn't cost anything, and you can easily incorporate extra walking into your daily life. Get off the bus or train one stop earlier than usual and walk the rest of the way home. Park your car some distance away from where you are going and walk the rest of the journey. Never take a lift, always walk.

Test the treatment yourself by taking a walk in fresh air five times a week for four weeks. Then cut out your daily walk for four weeks. Write down in a diary how you feel at the end of each week for the full eight weeks.

Be sociable

One of the early signs of depression is a reclusive tendency in which you no longer want to see friends or join in social activities. Many forms of exercise and sport are sociable and friendly and this is of undoubted value if you suffer from depression.

3

YOU REALLY NEED TO KNOW

◆ Sun, light and good air quality are essential for optimum mental and physical health.

◆ Endorphins—the feel-good hormones—are released during exercise and continue to make us feel good for some time after the exercise has stopped.

Exercise

Chapter

4

LIVING WITH DEPRESSION

On diagnosis

DOs AND DON'Ts

✓ Accept the diagnosis of depression, then make a plan for living.

✗ You don't have to tell other people of the diagnosis if you do not wish to.

Many people experience a sense of disbelief followed by overwhelming relief when depression is diagnosed. At least now there is an explanation for feeling so at odds with the world and yourself. Living with depression is neither easy nor enjoyable but it is manageable. The first step is to accept the diagnosis and the next is to consider a plan for living.

Dealing with immediate problems

◆ Get your prescription completed by the pharmacy and start taking your medication without delay.

◆ Do anything else you need to do that is directly related to your recovery, such as making appointments.

◆ If you are employed, you will need to tell your employers that you are ill and give them a date on which you are likely to return to work. You will need to supply a certificate from your doctor.

◆ If you are self-employed, you may need to reschedule some of your work and, if you have no alternative, such as sub-contracting, to turn down some jobs. You should check what state benefits are available.

◆ If you are at home looking after children, don't worry too much about housework for the time-being. Just concentrate on getting the children fed, washed, to school and to bed at a regular time.

◆ Basic survival: eating and sleeping are all you need to do if you cannot cope with anything else for now.

Overcoming the stigma

Many people suffer brief, recurrent episodes of depression and some suffer with moderate to severe depression throughout their lives. Depression affects as many as one in five people at some time in their lives. It

YOUR LIFE CAMPAIGN

◆ Dealing with specific and immediate problems

◆ Arranging medical appointments and any other matters directly concerned with your recovery

◆ Arranging for time off work or family duties

◆ Deciding who to tell

◆ Looking after your partner and family

◆ Setting your medium-term targets

◆ Setting your long-term goals

◆ Being realistic

◆ Working on long-term problems, such as anxiety, self-esteem, fatigue, weight gain or weight loss

◆ Choosing a lifestyle therapy

◆ Spotting the signs and seeking help if depression recurs

YOU REALLY NEED TO KNOW

◆ Very many people suffer with depression. Someone who lives in your road, someone else at your place of work and several other parents at your child's school will all suffer with depression at some time.

◆ Accepting the diagnosis is the first step towards recovery.

is therefore remarkable that some stigma over mental illness still remains. It is your personal choice who you tell and who you don't. If you believe that, in some instances, it is wiser to produce an explanation such as exhaustion, bronchitis or back pain, for example, then do so. It is entirely your decision and if you either can't or don't want to tell others, don't. However, the more people who are prepared to reveal that they have suffered from depression, the more acceptable it will become until the stigma is finally lost.

On diagnosis

Your partner and family

DOs AND DON'Ts

✓ Think back to happier times and recall things that you and your family did that gave you pleasure.

✗ Don't risk losing a valued relationship through your own thoughtlessness and anger.

We look to, and often get, support and sympathy in times of distress from those closest to us. However, it is difficult to live with someone who is always depressed and it would be wise to expect no more of your partner and family than of anyone else you know. Indeed, your partner may feel to blame. It is also natural to express any anger to those to whom we are closest and with whom we feel safest. That is difficult for those who love us to tolerate. However bad you feel, do and say what you can to show that you appreciate and love your partner and family. Sometimes this is not easy because depression can blunt loving feelings.

It has been said that happiness is having someone to love, something to do and something to look forward to. Loving someone and being loved is of inestimable value

YOUR GOALS

Look at the pie chart and consider how much of yourself and your time you are giving to each of the areas in your life. With the results of the pie chart in front of you, list the goals that you would like to achieve in each area of your life

YOUR WORK LIFE
What you do for a living, the work you do at home and the jobs (paid or unpaid) that you carry out for other people

YOUR FAMILY LIFE
Your time spent with your partner, family and friends

YOUR PERSONAL LIFE
The time that you have solely for yourself

and yet, sadly, some relationships break down under the strain of depression just when their succour and warmth is most needed. Many psychiatrists and other healthcare professionals believe that a good relationship is the key to happiness and success in the other fields of life.

If you have a relative who is depressed, you can help by showing her you care, sending cards, telephoning for a chat, doing little things for her and showing that you understand something of what she is going through.

Your goals

You may feel that now is an appropriate time to take a long, hard look at your life and reassess your goals and priorities, your thoughts and beliefs. Do you have a good balance in your life?

◆ Who and what is important to you, so that you can use your time in a rewarding and effective way.

◆ Everyone needs time exclusively for themselves in which to do whatever they wish.

◆ The three most important goals in life for you.

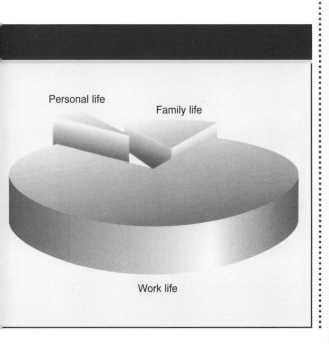

Personal life

Family life

Work life

Setting targets

✓ Check your diary or notebook every few days to make sure that you are on target for realizing your ambitions.

✗ On occasions when you feel really awful, don't get up. Staying in bed now and again will do you good.

Two of the most devastating aspects of depression are the loss of motivation and the despair. It takes energy and drive even to think of identifying goals and setting targets to achieve them when you are feeling depressed. However, as soon as you feel able, this step is a necessary part of recovery and an essential element of living with the hazard of recurrent depression.

Buy a diary or an exercise book and note your ambitions in the three areas of your life. No matter how far fetched something seems, write it down. You can consider later whether your choices are realistic. Each time you add something to the book, date it.

All ambitions and achievements are made up of small but significant steps. To take the first step, you need to identify your ambitions. Then you need to identify the steps required to bring you closer to your ambition. Let's say you want to learn to play the piano. You will need a piano, music books and a teacher. The cheapest way to go about this is to contact your local adult education

SETTING ACHIEVABLE GOALS

When you have decided on a realistic goal, break it down into a series of smaller goals to be achieved in stages.

◆ Whether you want to paint a room or write a novel, start with a plan.

◆ Divide the task into smaller steps—doors, ceiling, walls and windows or pages and chapters.

◆ Reward yourself as each step is accomplished.

LOOKING BACK AT YOUR GOALS

◆ Do you feel that you have a good balance of work and pleasure in your life? What do you wish to achieve in your work life? Where do you see yourself in five years' time?

◆ What do you wish to achieve emotionally, spiritually and materially for your family and home?

◆ What are the activities on which you would like to spend time? For example, reading, singing, going to the cinema, picture framing, dance, your favourite sport, walking.

◆ You can realize many of your ambitions. Take the first steps now.

◆ Achieving any step towards realizing your ambitions, however small, is another step towards recovery.

institute and enrol for a suitable course. Another way would be to find a private teacher. You can find one through local advertisements, the Yellow Pages or by word of mouth. You can use the same sorts of methods for finding out about any activity.

As another example, let's say that you wish to lose weight. There are two rules: eat smaller amounts of less fattening foods and exercise more. (See pp. 64–7.)

Being realistic

It is important that your ambitions are realistic. A 40-year-old woman is unlikely to become a supermodel and a 40-year-old man even less likely to become a football star. It is also important to remember that depression is a normal response to a sad life event. What is crucial is the severity, duration, degree of disablement and to what extent your behaviour is affected: it is when depression is severe, lengthy and prevents you from fully functioning that you need treatment.

Setting targets

59

Long-term problems

DOs AND DON'Ts

✓ Keep to a routine for eating, washing and sleeping.

✗ Don't be afraid to ask a friend, a member of the family or your doctor for help.

Depression is a complex illness with a number of different faces and not everyone shows the same symptoms. Some people, for example, appear to be suffering more from anxiety than depression.

Living with anxiety

Symptoms of anxiety include hypervigilance, severe tension, panic attack, perceived danger, phobia and phobic avoidance, doubt, insecurity and performance fears. Depression features physical slowness, sadness, perceived loss, loss of interest, despair, poor self-esteem, loss of libido, early morning waking and weight loss. However, anxiety often accompanies depression. It is important to try to reduce your anxiety levels.

If anxiety becomes disabling, you are no longer living your life fully and perceive constraints in every area of it. Relaxation techniques and cognitive or behavioural therapy (see pp. 43–4) are the best treatments.

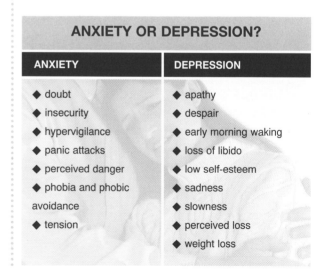

ANXIETY OR DEPRESSION?

ANXIETY	DEPRESSION
◆ doubt	◆ apathy
◆ insecurity	◆ despair
◆ hypervigilance	◆ early morning waking
◆ panic attacks	◆ loss of libido
◆ perceived danger	◆ low self-esteem
◆ phobia and phobic avoidance	◆ sadness
◆ tension	◆ slowness
	◆ perceived loss
	◆ weight loss

REDUCE YOUR ANXIETY LEVELS

You will not be able to do all these things, but doing just a few will start to improve your outlook on life.

◆ Take the first small steps to resolve long-term dilemmas.

◆ Make a list of all the things worrying you, then begin to deal with them. If you can manage to resolve just one each week, you will start to feel much better.

◆ Increase the amount of exercise you take.

◆ Try to ensure that you eat at least three times a day—and never skip breakfast.

◆ Go to bed one hour earlier than you normally do.

◆ Take time out for activities that you enjoy, such as flying a kite, squash, cinema, reading, watching a football match.

◆ Listen to a relaxation tape while breathing deeply.

Obsessive-compulsive ideas

Some people suffering with depression also develop signs of perfectionism that may border on obsessive-compulsive ideas—excessive checking, cleaning, washing and list-making and disabling procrastination. This behaviour, which also damages your self-esteem, can be described as a manifestation of anxiety and can be treated in the same way. If obsessive-compulsive tendencies start to encroach on your normal life, you should seek help in the form of medication and therapy through your family doctor.

◆ Try not to let things go. If you cannot cope with your finances, for example, ask a relative or friend to help you with checking your bank statements and paying your bills.

◆ Some kinds of anti-depressants act fast to relieve anxiety and ease tension.

◆ If you show signs of obsessive-compulsive disorder, as well as depression, your doctor will be able to prescribe the type of anti-depressant that can help both conditions

Long-term problems

Long-term solutions

✓ **Take action if you feel tired all the time—this may be a sign of poor self-esteem, anxiety and depression.**

✗ **No one can stay awake night after night. You will sleep when you teach yourself to relax.**

Try not to diminish or demean yourself in conversation with friends and colleagues. If you have a low opinion of yourself and your abilities, how can you expect anyone else to hold a good opinion? (See below.)

Resolving fatigue

Constant tiredness is a debilitating and common aspect of depression. It may even be the first symptom you notice. It is important for your recovery that you take steps to reduce it. Firstly, run through the measures for reducing anxiety (see p. 60). Secondly, ensure that you get good-quality sleep (see p. 63). Thirdly, eat healthily (see pp. 64–5). Fatigue will disappear within a fortnight.

FEELING GOOD ABOUT YOURSELF

IMPROVING SELF-ESTEEM

◆ Make every day count: do at least one thing that you are proud of and happy with.

◆ Telephone a close friend for a chat.

◆ List your good points and ask a close friend to add to it for you: you can think of least six positive elements.

◆ Accept yourself as you are: you cannot turn yourself into someone else. Concentrate on your good points.

◆ Say no when you need to: you don't have to do everything that is asked of you.

◆ Choose your friends: if you are unhappy within any of your relationships, make changes.

Sleep

These are the golden rules for good-quality sleep.

◆ Ensure you have a comfortable and supportive bed.

◆ Go to bed at roughly the same time each night.

◆ Get up at roughly the same time each morning.

◆ Make sure that there is nothing to keep you awake in the bedroom, such as books, a television or a radio.

◆ Make sure that the room is well ventilated.

◆ Make sure that the room is dark.

◆ Make sure that the room is quiet.

◆ If you cannot sleep, lie quietly in the dark and do your best to relax (see pp. 68–9).

◆ Take a warm bath just before bedtime.

AFFIRMATIONS

Choose the ones that appeal and repeat to yourself at intervals throughout the day.

◆ I can do this.

◆ I have something to offer people.

◆ People like me because I'm vivacious/eccentric/reliable/considerate/imaginative/intelligent/kind—you choose.

◆ I have attractive eyes/hair/body/hands.

◆ I am getting better day by day.

◆ I am good at mending things/carpentry/sewing/ironing/interior design/political debate/golf—you choose.

YOU REALLY NEED TO KNOW

◆ Low self-esteem amounts to a prejudice against yourself: avoid shooting yourself in the foot.

◆ It is often the things we haven't done that we regret, rather than those we do. If in doubt, go for it.

◆ Professional help is available through your family doctor to enable you to express any troubling thoughts and deal with them.

Long-term solutions

Eating for health

DOs AND DON'Ts

✓ You can use scales or a tape measure, but the BMI is the best way to assess whether your weight is healthy.

✗ Don't drink or at least cut down on alcohol, and reduce your caffeine intake, but be aware that withdrawal of caffeine can cause headaches and alcohol withdrawal can cause irritability and disturbed sleep for a week or two.

As depression disrupts our body systems and disturbs the appetite, it is important to pay extra attention to eating healthily and well. All you need to do is eat from the four main food groups and observe the golden rules. As a result, you will have much more energy, your skin will be improved, your hair will be glossier and you will feel better mentally, emotionally and physically.

You can check that your weight is at a healthy limit for your height by calculating your Body Mass Index. To do this, note your weight in kilograms and divide the number by your height in metres, squared. For example if your weight is 65 kg, and height 1.68 metres, first multiply 1.68 x 1.68 = 2.82 (your height squared). Next, divide 65 by 2.82. Your BMI is 23.

Most health care professionals agree that a BMI of 20–25 is healthy. Below 20 is regarded as underweight, over 25 is regarded as overweight, over 30 is obese and over 40 is a serious hazard to health.

THE FOUR FOOD GROUPS

Variety is the key to a balanced diet. Eat a selection from each of these food groups daily.

GROUP ONE	GROUP TWO	GROUP THREE	GROUP FOUR
◆ Meat	◆ Eggs	◆ Raw and cooked vegetables	◆ Wholegrain cereals
◆ Poultry	◆ Milk and milk products, such	◆ Raw and cooked fruit	◆ Rice
◆ Fish	as yogurt	◆ Fruit juice	◆ Wholemeal bread
◆ Dried or canned pulses	◆ Cheese	◆ Dried fruit	◆ Wholemeal pasta
◆ Tofu	◆ Nuts and seeds		

The golden rules

◆ Never eat in a hurry.

◆ Don't eat more than you need.

◆ Always drink water with a meal.

◆ Never skip breakfast.

◆ Never embark on a faddy or gimmicky diet.

◆ Don't go for meal replacements in any form.

◆ Don't crash diet.

◆ Don't miss meals.

◆ Don't ever go on a fast.

◆ Ignore cravings and give up highly processed and junk foods.

◆ Cut down on alcohol or stop drinking.

◆ Don't go shopping when you are hungry—eat first.

◆ Eating four, five or even six small meals a day is much better for your body than two or three larger meals a day.

◆ If you want to lose weight, cut down the size of portions and avoid foods high in fats or sugar.

◆ If you are overweight, don't buy larger size clothes.

◆ If you wish to gain weight, increase the size of portions and eat healthily from all four food groups every day.

◆ If you are underweight, don't take in your clothes or buy a smaller size.

◆ Eat slowly and don't try and do something else, such as reading or watching television, while you are eating: focus on the pleasure of the food.

◆ Try not to resort to convenience foods: cooking even a simple meal gives a lot of satisfaction.

◆ Finish your evening meal at least three hours before bedtime and drink water or a soft drink rather than tea, coffee or alcohol during the rest of the evening.

YOU REALLY NEED TO KNOW

◆ Avoid added salt, sugar, convenience meals, crisps, salted nuts, sweets, chocolate, biscuits, cakes, rich puddings, full cream, alcohol, greasy take-away meals. Cut down on tea and coffee and substitute with water or fruit juice.

◆ You will feel much better on a healthy balanced diet within days of starting it.

◆ For optimum health, you need to drink eight glasses of water a day. This is the ultra natural detox diet.

Eating for health

The feel-good factor

WHEN NOT TO

Don't exercise if you have a cold, infection or any illness.

Don't push yourself too hard or set unrealistic targets so that failing to meet them adds to your depression.

Don't exercise in very hot weather, as you may quickly become dehydrated.

Don't use apparatus in a gym or health club without taking the trainer's advice.

Don't exercise with persistent pain; consult your family doctor about it.

Exercise is vital for anyone suffering from depression, both during the illness and after recovery. Its effects on the body are a powerful force in keeping depression away. Recent research has shown the benefits of the release of the feel-good hormones that are associated with vigorous exercise. Increased energy levels when you exercise regularly will make you feel marvellous. Exercise causes blood sugar to rise and so you are less likely to lack energy, feel hungry and eat sugary snacks.

The heart, the most important muscle of the body, grows stronger and larger with exercise and so can pump more oxygenated blood to the muscles with less effort and fewer beats. This reduces strain on the heart.

When you are unfit, the heart has to work harder and beat much faster to pump the required amount of blood through the system and waste products stay in the body for longer. This can lead to the formation of deposits in the arteries which impede the flow of freshly oxygenated blood to all parts of the body. The heart then has to work even harder to overcome this resistance and so blood pressure is raised and more strain put on the body.

Exercise is both a lifestyle choice and an additional method of treatment (see pp. 50–1).

Ridding the body of toxins

Exercise is vital for the elimination of toxic waste from the body. It stimulates the whole body to function more efficiently and quickly so that waste products are excreted without delay. You may have a few aches and pains in the first few days of exercise as your muscles become accustomed to new challenges. Muscles may ache temporarily as they yield up long-stored lactic acid waste product. These few aches will soon disappear.

EXERCISES FOR LIFE

EXERCISE FOR CHILDREN

- Climbing frame
- Cycling
- Flying a kite
- Football
- Frisbee
- Ice skating
- Riding
- Rollerblading
- Skipping
- Squash
- Table tennis
- Tennis
- Tobogganing
- Walking

EXERCISE FOR PREGNANT WOMEN

- Aerobics
- Aquarobics
- Dance class
- Stretch and tone class
- Swimming
- Walking
- Yoga

EXERCISE FOR THE OVER-60s

- Badminton
- Bowling
- Cycling
- Golf
- Rambling and walking
- Swimming
- T'ai chi
- Yoga

YOU REALLY NEED TO KNOW

- Regular, sustained exercise is a treatment as well as a vital lifestyle choice for those who suffer with depression.

- Always drink a glass of water shortly before you intend to start exercising and again shortly after you have finished.

- For maximum health, avoid these toxins: junk food, sugar, added salt, nicotine, caffeine and alcohol.

The feel-good factor

Lifestyle therapies

DOs AND DON'Ts

✓ Everyone—depressed or not—benefits from some form of complete relaxation. Do learn one of these techniques.

✗ Don't look on relaxation as a chore to be completed— you will only add to your depression.

Some complementary therapies have the same function as exercise—they are both a treatment and a way to enhance your lifestyle. The next few pages describe a selection of those that are particularly suited for treating depression and anxiety. They are also beneficial to those with manic depression and postnatal depression.

Meditation for relaxation

The deep relaxation and increased mental clarity that meditation brings relieve anxiety and depression.

◆ Lie on your back on the floor in a quiet, comfortable place. Put a cushion under your neck. The palms of your hands should be outstretched and facing up.

◆ Close your eyes and consciously relax your whole body, one part at a time.

HOW TO TAKE YOUR OWN PULSE

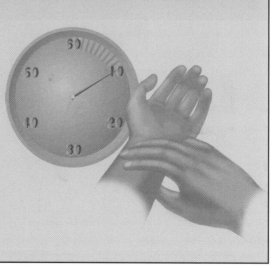

The rate at which the heart beats varies with age, activity and anxiety. Feel for the pulse at the wrist of one hand just below the base of the thumb. Place three fingers on it and press lightly. Do not use your thumb. Count the beats for 30 seconds, then double the number. The average pulse rate for a man at rest is 60–80 beats per minute and for a woman 78–82. In the elderly it may drop to as low as 60.

◆ Concentrate on your feet and toes. Let them relax. Now focus upon your legs, concentrating on relaxing first your calves and then your knees and thighs.

◆ Make sure your spine is supple and relaxed with your shoulders as opened out as possible and flat on the floor. Let your arms go and relax your hands.

◆ Concentrate on your breathing. Feel your abdominal muscles become more relaxed as your breathing deepens and slows.

◆ Let your mind float. Feel your worries floating away out of your body. Allow your spirit to relax. Remain like this for up to 20 minutes, without going to sleep.

◆ Get up slowly and stretch out your limbs, one by one, and then your back.

Visualization for relaxation

With this therapy, you can choose to focus on positive images and the desired outcome to specific situations. This allows you to cope with your problems and see your way through your depression and eventually to fulfil your potential. What you visualize can become the reality.

◆ Sit in a comfortable chair or lie on your back on the floor and close your eyes. You may find that you can also do this on a train or bus journey.

◆ Imagine a scene that spells peace and tranquillity— the moors, a seascape or mountains. What matters is that its message is quiet and relaxing.

◆ Allow yourself to be drawn into your picture and to exclude everything else in your life.

◆ Now visualize a specific situation and allow your mind the freedom to find the desired outcome, the resolution. Explore different ideas.

◆ When you get up, do so slowly.

YOU REALLY NEED TO KNOW

◆ Combating anxiety is a foundation for recovering from depression, panic attacks and phobia.

◆ A hypnotherapist can teach you the principles of hypnosis and auto-hypnosis so that you can use the techniques at home.

◆ It is extremely helpful to be able to monitor your level of anxiety at any time and in any situation. Taking your own pulse and using biofeedback are ways of doing this.

Complementary therapies

DOs AND DON'Ts

✓ Try some or all these therapies to find out if an invigorating or relaxing therapy works best for you.

✗ Don't abandon the therapy you have chosen when your depression eases. Keep it as a lifestyle therapy to help prevent recurrence.

The Alexander Technique

Mastering this gives you an powerful tool for dealing with anxiety and depression. The Technique teaches people how to adopt the correct posture for all daily activities, which helps them develop an awareness of their bodies and how they move. By correcting their posture, they can avoid some of the aches and pains that are common in depression. Lessons in the Technique are usually given individually and you can then use it on your own.

Massage

This is probably one of the most deliciously luxurious complementary therapies—even more so when combined with the aromatherapy oils of your choice.

DO-IT-YOURSELF MASSAGE

FACE

With the tips of your first two fingers, make small circles over your face from the jaw, up the cheeks and over the temples. Repeat with slow palm strokes.

FOOT

Stroke along the length of your foot sandwiched between your palms. Rub the heel vigorously. Then make small circles over the sole with your thumb.

NECK

Wrap one hand, palm downwards across the nape of your neck. Lightly pinch the muscles between thumb and index finger, then knead them gently.

You can learn the chief techniques at evening classes or have massage therapy in some beauty salons, homeopathic clinics, naturopathic clinics and health spas. Professional massage is deeply relaxing and at the same time profoundly invigorating for it helps eliminate toxins through stimulating lymph drainage channels.

If you are going to use essential oils, choose soothing ones such as frankincense, geranium, lavender, neroli, rose, violet or ylang-ylang. Dilute them well with a carrier oil, such as sunflower or safflower.

Colour therapy

It has been well documented that certain colours bring out certain moods. The theory of colour therapy is that the body absorbs colour in the form of electromagnetic components of light and then produces its own aura of electromagnetism. This gives off a pattern of vibrations that can be discerned by a trained colour therapist. An unhealthy body and mind produces an unbalanced pattern of vibrations. The colour therapist seeks to administer the colour or colours that the sick person lacks in order to restore balance and harmony. Both depression and anxiety in its many forms can respond well to colour therapy.

Chiropractic and osteopathy

These manipulative therapies are especially valuable for treating not only depression and anxiety but also their physical manifestations, such as headache, neck ache and back pain. Both manipulate the spine in order to alleviate physical stresses, eliminate toxins and boost flagging energy levels. Both these therapies often create a deep sense of well-being and relaxation.

◆ The spine holds our skeleton together and when it is out of alignment or in pain, our emotional and physical health are compromised.

◆ Mind and body are inextricably linked.

Complementary therapies

DOs AND DON'Ts

✓ Do make sure you find a qualified professional practitioner.

✗ Don't forget to mention any of your symptoms, as the therapist needs the full picture.

Hydrotherapy

Any therapy associated with water is likely to benefit people suffering from depression for water has uniquely calming properties. Hydrotherapy techniques boost circulation, which increases energy levels and rids the body of the toxins acquired through the erratic eating habits and sluggish lifestyle characteristic of depression.

Dance therapy

Research into which types of exercise most benefit people who suffer with depression shows Scottish country dancing at the top of the league. Psychologists believe that the combination of vigorous exercise, music and smiling combine to raise endorphin levels to an enviable high. It is very likely that other types of dance, notably South American dance, jazz dance and jive, will bring about similar benefits.

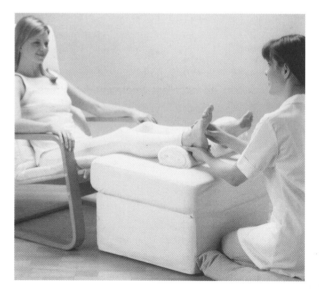

Reflexology is a form of specialist foot massage. With firm pressure from the thumb, the reflexologist stimulates specific points on the sole of the foot that are connected via the nervous system to the body's major organs.

HERBALISM

A medical herbalist can decide which herbs will benefit you and may prescribe an infusion, decoction or tincture.

HERBS USED FOR DEPRESSION AND ANXIETY

◆ St John's wort (*Hypericum perforatum*)

◆ Borage and vervain teas

◆ Infusion of lavender tops

◆ Tea of finely chopped poplar bark and gentian root with a little added agrimony and centaury

◆ Rosemary tea

◆ Infusion of lemon balm leaves

◆ Infusion of equal parts of skullcap and vervain

◆ Ginseng tea

Acupuncture

One of the chief elements of traditional Chinese medicine, acupuncture is now increasingly accepted in the West. It is an excellent treatment for stress and anxiety, and tends to make people feel better. The acupuncturist painlessly inserts small sterilized needles—they range from 7mm to 50mm long—at key points on your body, situated along 12 meridians.

Reflexology

The practitioner works on the relevant meridian points in the feet for depression and anxiety, so that you feel lighter and more relaxed in mood, more energetic and free from aches and pains.

YOU REALLY NEED TO KNOW

◆ Complementary therapies share the ability to reduce anxiety, boost flagging energy levels and induce a profound sense of well-being.

◆ There are other alternative therapies which may be helpful, such as acupressure, autogenic training and art therapy.

Will it happen again?

✓ If you experience any of the familiar symptoms of depression, consult your family doctor.

✓ Write down how you feel when you are ill, so that you can refer to it if necessary in the future.

✓ Try to keep a balance in all aspects of your life—work, family and your own needs.

Some people experience an episode of depression once only in their lives and never again. For the majority, however, depression is a chronic (recurrent) illness. It is wise therefore to bear these guidelines in mind.

Life guidelines

◆ Be careful not to allow too much stress into your life, for this can trigger depression.

◆ When you are, unavoidably, going through a stressful period, make sure that you eat, sleep and exercise regularly so that you can counteract some of the adverse effects.

◆ Take extra care of yourself during and after illness for this is when you may be most vulnerable.

◆ Always keep a balance in your life between your work life, your home life and your personal time.

FACTS AND FIGURES

◆ More than half the people who have one attack of depression necessitating treatment will have at least one further episode of depression at some time in their lives.

◆ About one-quarter of patients relapse within one year and three-quarters will experience a recurrence within ten.

◆ Depression is twice as common in women as in men.

◆ More than one-third (37 percent) of people treated for depression by primary care physicians suffer recurrent depression within 19 months.

◆ Women who have had one episode of puerperal psychosis (see p.13) have a 50 percent chance of recurrence.

◆ The more severe the first depression and the greater the number of episodes, the greater the probability of relapse.

ILL AND/OR DEPRESSED

◆ Don't forget that you can be ill as well as depressed. Some conditions, such as flu and high blood pressure, may produce symptoms similar to those of depression.

◆ Because some of the symptoms of depression coincide with the symptoms of other conditions, it may be that you are not suffering from depression at all.

◆ Take care not to attribute all illness to depression at the risk of neglecting your physical health.

YOU REALLY NEED TO KNOW

◆ Depression can often recur.

◆ You can reduce the possibility of another attack of depression.

◆ You can and will get well again.

◆ Depression does not confer immunity from all other illnesses, so feeling unwell may be owing to a physical illness, not depression.

◆ Depression can trigger important and positive changes in your life.

Write down your own particular set of symptoms and how you feel when you are depressed, so that when you are better, you can refer to it if necessary. It is not easy for us to spot a recurrence of the illness in ourselves, because we tend to forget how things were when we were ill and because, when we start to fall ill again, we lose insight into our own condition.

The winning card

This chapter has been dedicated to living with depression from the time of diagnosis onwards, how to help yourself and how to prevent a recurrence. The measures, which include coping with anxiety and adopting a healthy lifestyle towards eating, sleeping and exercising, are absolutely essential for reducing the likelihood of a recurrence of depressive illness. Don't ignore these vital measures: you hold all the trump cards for improving the quality and direction of your life. All you have to do is play them.

Understanding the jargon

When your depression is first diagnosed, you are likely to have to learn a whole new vocabulary so that you will understand what your medical advisers are telling you. It will take time to absorb all the new information, but you will be surprised at how quickly you start to use these terms and how they no longer seem strange.

ANXIOLYTICS—anti-anxiety drugs, also known as tranquillizers. Some types are addictive.

BEHAVIOURAL THERAPY—a programme of exposing someone with a phobia to the source of fear in a series of gradual steps.

BIPOLAR DISORDER—manic depression.

COGNITIVE THERAPY—a talking therapy designed to identify and challenge negative thought patterns.

DOPAMINE—a monoamine chemical in the brain associated with gaining pleasure.

ECT—electroconvulsive therapy is a treatment in which an electric current is passed through the brain to induce a short fit. It is used to treat severe recurrent depression.

INTERPERSONAL THERAPY—a talking therapy aimed at improving personal relationships and modifying a depressed person's perceptions.

MAOIS—monoamine oxidase inhibitors are a family of anti-depressants that slows down the removal of monoamines by the enzyme monoamine oxidase.

MELATONIN—a hormone derived from serotonin. Raised levels, owing to lack of sunlight, may cause SAD.

MONOAMINES—a group of chemicals in the brain, which includes serotonin, dopamine and noradrenaline.

NEUROTRANSMITTERS—chemicals involved in the transmission of nerve impulses; chemical messengers.

NORADRENALINE—a monoamine chemical in the brain involved in regulating mood and energy.

PSYCHIATRIST—medical doctor with an additional psychiatric qualification.

PSYCHOSIS—severe mental disorder in which contact with reality is extremely distorted.

PSYCHOTHERAPY—various therapies designed to modify a depressed person's feelings, views and ideas of self through sympathetic, directive discussion.

SAD—Seasonal Affective Disorder, a biological effect of low light levels in winter that causes depression.

SEROTONIN—a monoamine chemical in the brain that maintains normal patterns of appetite, sleep and sexual activity and is thought to influence mood. It is also called 5-hydroxytryptamine or 5HT.

SSRIs—selective serotonin reuptake inhibitors are a family of anti-depressants that raise serotonin levels in the brain. The best known are Prozac and Seroxat (Paxil in the USA).

TCAs—tricyclic anti-depressant family that corrects a deficiency of monamines.

UNIPOLAR ILLNESS—classic depression

Where to go for help

USEFUL ADDRESSES

APNI ASSOCIATION FOR POST NATAL ILLNESS
25 Jerdan Place
London SW6 1BE
0207 386 0868

CRUSE BEREAVEMENT CARE
Cruse House
126 Sheen Rd
Richmond
Surrey TW9 1UR
020 8940 4818

DEPRESSION ALLIANCE
35 Westminster Bridge Rd
London SE1 7JB
020 7633 0557

MDF – MANIC DEPRESSION FELLOWSHIP
8-10 High St
Kingston
Surrey KT1 1EY
Helpline 020 7793 2600

MIND (NATIONAL ASSOCIATION FOR MENTAL HEALTH)
MindinfoLine: 0345 660163

NATIONAL CHILDBIRTH TRUST
Alexandra House
Oldham Terrace
London W3 6NH
020 8992 8637

RELATE (NATIONAL MARRIAGE GUIDANCE)
01788 573241

ROYAL COLLEGE OF PSYCHIATRISTS
17 Belgrave Square
London SW1X 8PG
020 7235 2351

SADA – SEASONAL AFFECTIVE DISORDER ASSOCIATION
P O Box 989
Steyning
W Sussex
Helpline: 01903 814942

FURTHER READING

Anxiety and Depression: Your Questions Answered Professor Cosmo Hallstrom and Dr Nicola McClure (Churchill Livingstone, Edinburgh, 1998)

Cognitive Therapy of Depression Aaron T Beck, A John Rush, Brian F Shaw and Gary Emery (Guilford Press, New York, 1979)

Darkness Visible William Styron (Jonathan Cape, London, 1991)

Growing up Sad: Childhood Depression and Its Treatment Leon Cytryn and Donald McKnew (Norton, New York, 1998)

Malignant Sadness: The Anatomy of Depression Lewis Wolpert (Faber, London, 1999)

Mind Over Mood: Change How You Feel by Changing the Way You Think Dennis Greenberger and Christine A Padesky (Guilford Press, New York, 1995)

The Many Faces of Depression edited by Professor Malcolm Lader and Dr Alan Wade (The Royal Society of Medicine Press, London, 1999)

Index

Index

Acknowledgements

SPL= Science Photo Library

Photographs: 8/9 Hank Morgan/SPL; 19,46 BSIP Boucharlat/SPL;
20,47 James Prince/SPL; 22/23,28/29 Peter Menzel/SPL; 32/33,42,43 John Greim/SPL;
45 BSIP, LBL/SPL; 49 Pascal Goetgheluck/SPL; 50 Renee Lynn/SPL; 67 Jerry Wachter/SPL

This book was edited and designed by Axis Design Editions Limited,
8 Accommodation Road, London NW11 8ED

With gratitude to:
Chris Broadbent, Dr John Cutting, Dr Ann Dally, Ros Edlin, Dr Brian Gazzard, Mark
Hardcastle, Dr J. Hargreaves, Dr Frances Parrish, Anne Smith and Dr J. Taylor

OUGHBOROUGH COLLEGE LIBRARY